Breakthrough

Inventions

INVENTING THE ELECTRIC LIGHT

Lisa Mullins

Crabtree Publishing Company

www.crabtreebooks.com

Breakthrough Inventions

Crabtree Publishing Company
www.crabtreebooks.com

Coordinating editor: Ellen Rodger

Series and project editor: Adrianna Morganelli

Designer and production coordinator: Rosie Gowsell

Production assistant: Samara Parent

Scanning technician: Arlene Arch-Wilson

Art director: Rob MacGregor

Prepress technician: Nancy Johnson

Project development, editing, photo editing, and layout: First Folio Resource Group, Inc.: Tom Dart, Sarah Gleadow, Debbie Smith

Photo research: Maria DeCambra, Linda Tanaka

Consultants: Harold D. Wallace, Jr., Associate Curator in the Electricity Collections, The National Museum of American History

Photographs: Bettmann/Corbis: cover (center left), title page (top), copyright page, p. 5, p. 14 (bottom), p. 17 (top); Stefano Bianchetti/Corbis: p. 10; Bibliothèque des Arts Décoratifs, Paris, France/Archives Charmet/ Bridgeman Art Library: p. 4 (right); Ashley Cooper/Corbis: p. 28; Famous People Players: p. 29 (top); Granger Collection, New York: p. 9 (right), p. 15 (top), p. 16 (top), middle); istockphoto.com/gwmullis: p. 23 (top); istockphoto.com/Henrikroger: title page (bottom), contents page (bottom right); p. 23 (bottom); istockphoto.com/Justin Horrocks: contents page (middle right); istockphoto.com/icenine photography: contents page (bottom middle); istockphoto.com/Shaun Lowe: p. 21 (left); istockphoto.com/Sean McBride: p. 21 (right); istockphoto.com/Laura Neal: contents page (middle center); istockphoto.com/pederk: contents page (bottom left); istockphoto.com/Roger Pilkington: pp. 16–17 (bottom); istockphoto.com/ Norman Pogson: p. 24; istockphoto.com/Eline Spek: p. 25 (left);

istockphoto.com/Jack Tzekov: contents page (middle left); istockphoto.com/ Filipe Varela: p. 20 (top); istockphoto.com/Natthawat Wongrat: contents page (top); Peter Kneffel/dpa/Corbis: p. 31 (top); Andrew Lambert Photography/Science Photo Library: p. 7 (right); Lester Lefkowitz/Corbis: p. 27, James Leynse/Corbis: p. 13 (right); Liu Liqun/Corbis: p. 25 (right); Robert Llewellyn/Corbis: p. 30 (bottom); Mary Evans Picture Library: p. 9 (left); New York Public Library/Art Resource, NY: p. 4 (left); NiteRider®/ Dive Lights International, Inc.: p. 30 (top); Private Collection/Archives Charmet/The Bridgeman Art Library: p. 11 (left); Private Collection/ Bridgeman Art Library: p. 6; Private Collection/© Philip Mould, Historical Portraits Ltd, London, UK/Bridgeman Art Library: p. 12 (right); Roger Ressmeyer/Corbis: p. 29 (bottom); Schenectady Museum/Hall of Electrical History Foundation/Corbis: p. 18 (bottom), p. 19 (top), p. 20 (bottom), p. 26; Science Museum/Science & Society Picture Library: p. 8, p. 14 (top), p. 15 (bottom); Science Museum Library/Science & Society Picture Library: p. 19 (bottom); Science Photo Library: p. 7 (left), p. 13 (left); Smithsonian American Art Museum, Washington, DC/Art Resource, NY: p. 18 (top); Sheila Terry/Photo Researchers, Inc.: p. 12 (left); Other images from stock CD.

Cover: The invention of the electric light in the late 1800s changed the way people lived, worked, and were entertained. There are now many different types of electric lights, but the technology behind an ordinary incandescent light bulb is basically the same as it was in 1878.

Title page: Two scientists working separately — Joseph Swan, from England, and Thomas Edison, from the United States — developed the incandescent light bulb in the 1870s to light up indoor and outdoor spaces.

Contents page: Light bulbs in bright colors and interesting shapes are often used more for decoration than to light up spaces.

Library and Archives Canada Cataloguing in Publication

Mullins, Lisa, 1981-
    Inventing the Electric Light / Lisa Mullins.

(Breakthrough Inventions)
Includes index.
ISBN 978-0-7787-2818-4 (bound)
ISBN 978-0-7787-2840-5 (pbk.)

    1. Electric lighting--History--Juvenile literature.
2. Inventions--Juvenile literature. I. Title. II. Series.

TK4131.M84 2007   j621.32   C2007-900656-6

Library of Congress Cataloging-in-Publication Data

Mullins, Lisa, 1981-
    Inventing the Electric Light / written by Lisa Mullins.
        p. cm. -- (Breakthrough Inventions)
    Includes index.
    ISBN-13: 978-0-7787-2818-4 (rlb)
    ISBN-10: 0-7787-2818-8 (rlb)
    ISBN-13: 978-0-7787-2840-5 (pb)
    ISBN-10: 0-7787-2840-4 (pb)
    1. Electric lighting--History--Juvenile literature. I. Title. II. Series.

    TK4131.M85 2007
    621.3209--dc22   2007002922
                                                  LC

Crabtree Publishing Company

www.crabtreebooks.com   1-800-387-7650

Published in Canada
Crabtree Publishing
616 Welland Ave.
St. Catharines, ON
L2M 5V6

Published in the United States
Crabtree Publishing
PMB16A
350 Fifth Ave., Suite 3308
New York, NY 10118

Published in the United Kingdom
Crabtree Publishing
White Cross Mills
High Town, Lancaster
LA1 4XS

Published in Australia
Crabtree Publishing
386 Mt. Alexander Rd.
Ascot Vale (Melbourne)
VIC 3032

SOC

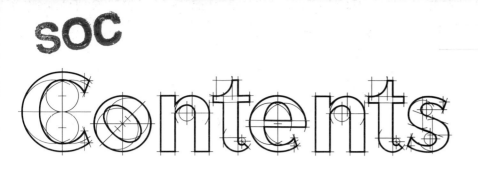

Early Lights

I lluminating, or lighting up, an area is easy. With the flick of a switch, lights go on. Today, most lights, including streetlights and lights in homes, are electric. They use electricity to heat up a metal, which produces light. Before the electric light was invented, people relied on the Sun, the Moon, and fire for light.

Controlling Fire

The Sun and Moon are sources of light, but humans cannot control when, or how brightly, they shine. When **prehistoric** humans discovered how to control fire, they not only used it to cook food, make tools, and stay warm, but as a source of light as well.

(right) Prehistoric people built fires to create light and heat, and cook food.

Fire Lights

Prehistoric people burned fires in pits in the ground and used fire in lamps made from hollow stones or large shells. They placed wood, leaves, moss, and tallow, or animal fat, inside and set it aflame. They also carried torches, or thick pieces of wood dipped in tallow or **resin** and set on fire, to travel more safely in the dark. The first candles were made more than 2,000 years ago by placing pieces of twisted or woven cloth in chunks of beeswax or tallow. Candles burned longer than torches, and were a common source of light until the 1900s.

(above) Many candles or torches were needed to light large rooms. The use of open flames indoors sometimes led to rooms accidentally catching fire.

Oil Lamps

Torches and candles could not provide enough light to illuminate large spaces well. By 100 A.D., the Romans were using oil lamps made from a type of clay called terra cotta and from certain metals, such as bronze. For fuel, the lamps burned animal and fish oils, as well as oil from vegetables, plants, and trees. Oil lamps burned for longer and provided a stronger and steadier light than candles, but they were still not very bright, often produced a lot of smoke, and gave off an unpleasant smell.

Around 1760, Paris, France, became the first city to illuminate its streets with oil lamps, replacing the candle lamps it had used before. A new type of oil, called kerosene, became popular in the 1850s. Kerosene is produced by burning coal, and it was easier and less expensive to produce than other oils.

Light Today

Today, electric lights are part of everyday life in most parts of the world, but not all. Some places, such as parts of Africa and central Asia, do not have electric lights because electricity is expensive to generate, or produce, as well as to buy. Fire and oil lamps, which are less expensive, are used instead. Other places do not have electric lighting systems due to extreme weather conditions. In Antarctica, for example, the cold causes power lines and machines used to generate electricity to break. The cost of maintaining lighting systems in these places is high.

(top) If most oil lamps were left burning for long, a thick layer of greasy black oil gradually covered the walls, furniture, and other surfaces of a room. Whale oil lamps, which only the wealthiest people could afford, did not smell or produce smoke.

First Experiments

E lectricity was not invented, it was discovered. The ancient Greeks and Romans knew that rubbing a piece of amber with certain materials, such as wool and fur, caused the amber to attract feathers and other lightweight objects, but they did not recognize this attraction as a form of electricity called static electricity.

Early Discoveries

William Gilbert was a famous English doctor and **philosopher** who conducted experiments in the late 1500s to find out how **magnetism** worked. Gilbert discovered that objects other than pieces of amber, such as diamonds, also attracted lightweight objects when rubbed with certain materials. In 1600, he named this power "electric," after the Greek word for amber, which is "elektron." Other scientists began experimenting with "electrics" and discovered positive and negative charges. By trial and error, they learned that objects with opposite charges attract each other, or stick together, while those with the same charge repel each other, or push each other away.

Experiments with Air Pumps

In the late 1600s, many scientists were investigating the nature of air by conducting experiments using air pumps. Around 1700, the English scientist Francis Hauksbee noticed that when a **barometer** was placed in an air pump that had been emptied of air, it glowed purple. Hauksbee wondered what this purple glow was and how it was produced.

William Gilbert is pictured here demonstrating his discoveries about "electrics" to England's Queen Elizabeth I.

The First Electrical Machine

After conducting more experiments, Hauksbee found that rubbing a wool cloth against a hollow glass tube made the tube glow purple, just like the barometer. Dust and feathers underneath the tube moved around, and some even stuck to the tube. Hauksbee realized that the things he was observing were caused by static electricity.

Hauksbee built the first electrical machine, or machine to generate static electricity, in 1705. It consisted of a large glass sphere placed on a metal rod with a handle. Turning the handle made the sphere spin very quickly. When Hauksbee held his hand against the spinning sphere, static electricity was created, and the sphere gave off a bright purple light. Hauksbee had accidentally created an electric light.

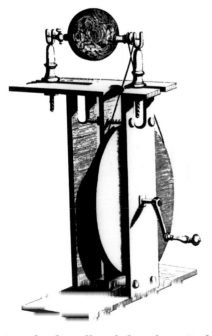

Turning the handle of the electrical machine quickly required a great deal of strength.

Static Electricity

All matter is made of tiny particles called atoms. Atoms contain protons, which are positively charged, and electrons, which are negatively charged. An atom with the same number of protons and electrons is neutral, or its charges are balanced.

Rubbing certain materials together can cause electrons to move from one material to another. A change in the number of electrons in a material creates a static electric charge. Materials that lose electrons become positively charged, and materials that gain electrons become negatively charged. Charged objects attract objects with the opposite charge. They also attract neutral objects. For example, when amber and wool are rubbed together, the amber gains electrons from the wool. The amber becomes negatively charged and attracts neutral materials, such as feathers.

Sometimes when hair is brushed, it sticks up. That is static electricity. The brush or comb gains electrons from the hair, and attracts it.

Stephen Gray

Stephen Gray was an English cloth dyer who experimented with static electricity. In 1705, Gray rubbed a wool cloth against a glass tube that had a cork in each end. He discovered that feathers were attracted to the corks instead of to the tube. Gray concluded that the glass tube had conducted, or carried, its electric charge to the corks.

Gray then began to test how far, and through what materials, electricity could travel. In one experiment, he strung 820 feet (250 meters) of wire around a garden. When he touched a rubbed glass tube to one end of the wire, feathers and small pieces of metal on the ground jumped up to the other end of the wire. The electricity had traveled the length of the wire.

The Leyden Jar

Until the mid-1700s, anyone who experimented with electricity had to generate it for each experiment, using static. In 1746, a university professor in Holland named Pieter van Musschenbroek accidentally discovered a way to store and transport electricity. His discovery was named the "Leyden jar" in honor of the university where he taught.

The Leyden jar was the first electrical capacitor. Capacitors allow electric charges to be stored and transported. Van Musschenbroek attached a metal wire to the metal rod on an electrical machine. The electrical charge from the machine traveled through the wire and into a glass jar of water, where the other end of the wire rested. The jar became electrically charged. Later, several jars were lined with lead foil instead of water, making them lighter and easier to transport.

Experimenters could carry the electrically charged jars to lecture halls for demonstrations, or from one laboratory to another for further experiments. Anyone who worked with the charged jars had to be careful not to touch the wire or the rod on the machine at the same time as they touched the jar. Those who did received an enormous shock that could knock them to the ground, make their noses bleed, or even cause them to faint.

A Leyden jar held its charge for several hours or even a whole day. It produced more powerful electric shocks and sparks than anything before it.

Benjamin Franklin

In 1752, American inventor Benjamin Franklin proposed a way to test the theory that lightning was electrical. He suggested making a silk kite with a wooden cross and a sharp, pointed wire on top. A metal key wrapped in silk would be attached to the kite's string to conduct the electricity, and the end of the kite's string would be placed in an uncharged Leyden jar. Franklin believed that, when the kite was flown in a storm, lightning would charge the jar. He was right, proving that lightning was the same kind of electricity that experimenters generated in their laboratories.

Historians are not certain whether Benjamin Franklin actually performed his kite experiment. It was very dangerous, and several men in Europe died from electric shock in the early 1750s while trying it.

In the 1740s, Antoine Nollet, an electrical experimenter from France, became known for his demonstration of jumping soldiers. A group of soldiers held hands. The soldier at one end touched the rod of an electrical machine, while the soldier at the other end placed his hand on a Leyden jar. An enormous shock was generated that caused all the soldiers to jump in the air at the same time.

Sparks and Shocks

Throughout the 1700s, experimenters and entertainers gave public demonstrations of their most spectacular experiments. Those who were interested in electricity tried to teach their audiences the basics of electrical science, but their main goal was to entertain and amaze. They made small lightning bolts flash from their fingertips by touching electrical machines, waved charged glass rods over feathers to make the feathers dance in the air, and set glasses of alcohol on fire by touching them with electrified metal swords. One of the most popular entertainments was the electric kiss. A man held an electrical machine, which gave him an electrical charge. He then kissed a woman, creating a small shock.

Current and Light

By the end of the 1700s, scientists could produce, store, and redirect static electricity. In the 1800s, the discovery of how to produce electricity in a continuous flow allowed electricity to be used to illuminate indoor and outdoor spaces more brightly than oil lamps and for longer periods of time.

Galvani's Frogs

Luigi Galvani was a professor of anatomy at the University of Bologna, in Italy. He was very interested in the anatomy of frogs, and performed hundreds of **dissections**. In 1786, he touched a pair of metal scissors to a dead frog's leg nerves during a thunder and lightning storm. To his surprise, the frog's leg moved. The same thing happened when Galvani pressed a copper hook into a dead frog's spinal cord, while the hook was hanging on an iron rail. Galvani concluded that the muscle twitching was related to "animal electricity," which, he argued, all animals had in their bodies. Most scientists accepted Galvani's ideas, but an Italian physics professor named Alessandro Volta was not convinced.

(top) Many visitors came to Luigi Galvani's anatomy laboratory, curious to see him make dead frogs "dance."

Alessandro Volta

Alessandro Volta believed that it was not "animal electricity" that caused the frogs' legs to twitch in Galvani's dissections, but electricity generated by the metal in the tools Galvani used. In the 1790s, Volta conducted experiments to test his theory. He discovered that putting two different metals together sometimes produced a very small electric charge. Silver and **zinc** produced the strongest charge. Volta piled pairs of metals on top of each other to see whether this would make the charge stronger, but it did not.

Volta's Pile

In 1800, Volta placed pieces of cardboard soaked in salt water between pairs of silver and zinc disks that were piled on top of each other. The wet cardboard was an excellent conductor. When Volta touched the top of the pile, he got a huge shock. When he touched the pile again a few minutes later, he got another large shock. Volta had created the first battery and steady current of electricity, though the current did not last for long.

Current Electricity

An electric current is a stream of electrons that is moving through a material. Electricity flows easily through electrical conductors, such as metals or the wet cardboard in Volta's pile. It does not flow easily through insulators, such as rubber.

Electric currents transfer electrical energy from one point to another. The current flows from one end of a source, usually a battery or generator, through a conductor, such as a metal wire, to the other end of the source. On a battery, the two ends are the negative and positive terminals. The complete path that the current travels is called a circuit. If a light bulb is placed in the middle of a circuit, it will stay lit as long as the flow of electricity is not interrupted.

An electric current causes atoms in the air to lose or gain electrons. These moving electrons release energy as light, which is the spark that appears between the wires.

Alessandro Volta demonstrated his pile, or battery, to many rulers in Europe, including Napoleon Bonaparte of France.

Incandescence

Scientists around the world, including English chemist Sir Humphry Davy, were fascinated by Volta's pile. Davy experimented with the pile, using different materials to try to produce an even stronger electric current. In 1801, he replaced the cardboard with **acid**, and later replaced one of the metals with **charcoal**. In 1803, Davy found that touching a strip of metal to one of his improved piles caused the metal to glow brightly. Davy had discovered that running a lot of electricity through a substance causes the substance to incandesce, or glow. This is known as the principle of incandescence.

(above) *In addition to his work on electricity, Sir Humphry Davy was a chemist who made important discoveries about heat, gases, and acids.*

Davy's Arc Lamp

In 1807, Davy used the principle of incandescence and his stronger pile to invent the first practical electric light. He set two charcoal rods a few inches apart, and attached each to the end of a pile with a wire. The current running from the pile was so strong that it caused the tips of the rods to incandesce, and an arc of electricity appeared between them. This created a bright white light in the shape of an arc, which remained until the rods of charcoal burned up.

(left) *Davy invented a safety lamp for miners, which could also detect dangerous gases. One way the miners knew there were gases is if the flame changed color.*

The new Paris Opera House, now known as the Opéra Garnier after its architect, was completed in 1874. It was one of the first public buildings to be built already wired for electric light.

Arc Lamps in Action

Arc lamps were very expensive, since the charcoal rods had to be replaced often. They were also very bright, and could not be made to shine less brightly. A number of wealthy people in North America and Europe tried to use arc lamps in their homes, but in such small spaces, the light hurt their eyes. Arc lamps were much more practical in larger spaces. In 1850, the Paris Opera House installed one of the first systems of electric arc lights, candles, and oil lamps. People walking by the opera house were amazed at the bright light coming from the windows, and audience members were surprised at how well they could see the performers on the stage. London, England, was one of the first cities to install outdoor arc lamps, in 1878. Soon, arc lamps illuminated streets across Europe. In the 1880s, cities in the American Midwest were lit with towers that had arc lights on top. More people went out at night, and shops, theaters, and restaurants stayed open later because of the improved lighting.

Arc Lamps Today

Arc lamps are still used today when very bright lights are needed. They are often used to illuminate movie sets, and in large film projectors to project movies onto screens. Arc lights are also used in searchlights, which help rescue workers and police search for missing people outside at night. Arc lamps no longer use charcoal. Instead, they use electrodes made of carbon, which are electrical conductors. An arc of light is produced between the two electrodes.

Arc lights provide the very bright light that is needed while filming movies and television programs.

Electric Light Bulbs

Throughout the 1800s, scientists and inventors conducted many experiments with arc lamps and incandescent light. They made further discoveries about what electricity was and how it worked. Two men working separately used this new information to invent the incandescent electric light bulb that we still use today.

Joseph Swan

Joseph Swan began experimenting with electric light bulbs in 1860. It was not until 1878 that he made an incandescent electric light bulb that stayed lit for more than a few minutes. Swan placed a small carbon rod from an arc lamp inside a glass bulb. Metal wires connected the bulb to an electrical generator. Electricity traveled from the generator through the wires and into the carbon rod, causing it to become hot enough to incandesce.

Usually, materials that become this hot catch fire and burn, but only if oxygen feeds the fire. Swan sealed his glass bulb and sucked out most of the air, which contains oxygen, creating a vacuum. This way, the rod lasted longer before it caught fire.

(above) Swan improved his light bulb by using a piece of thread soaked in acid instead of a small carbon rod. This allowed the bulb to burn longer.

(left) Joseph Swan received a British patent for his incandescent electric light bulb in 1878.

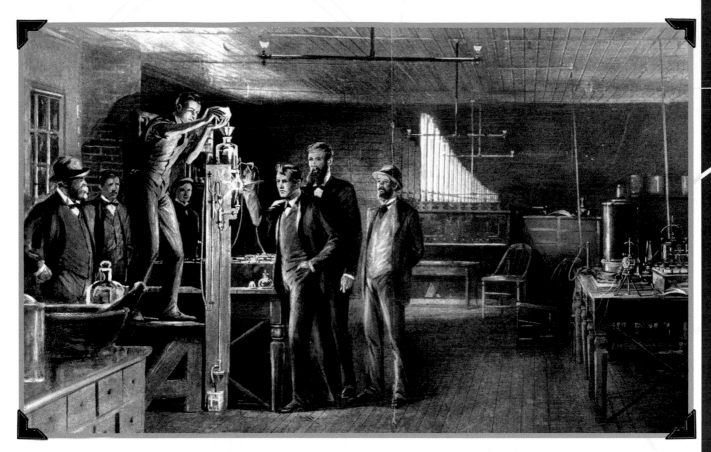

Edison's Light Bulb

Thomas Edison gets most of the credit for inventing the light bulb because the bulb he made lasted longer and was less expensive than Swan's light bulb. Edison also convinced people to use electric lights, and created a system for lighting entire cities and countries. In the 1870s, using the arc lamp as his model, Edison began experimenting with different "filaments," the word he used to describe the material inside the bulb that incandesces when electrified. In October 1879, after experimenting with hundreds of different filaments, Edison discovered that a **carbonized** cotton thread could stay lit for about 14 hours in an airless glass bulb. Soon after, Edison found that a piece of carbonized cardboard stayed lit even longer, for about 120 hours.

(right) Thomas Edison powered his light bulb with a generator, just as Joseph Swan did. Edison's light bulb was a different shape than Swan's because of the different filament Edison used.

(above) Thomas Edison spent months in his laboratory in Menlo Park, New Jersey, working on his electric light. He even slept there some nights.

Introducing Electric Lights

Edison immediately began building more light bulbs and new generators, and invented other devices to make his electrical lighting system work, such as **fuses**, sockets, and switches. On December 31, 1879, Edison opened the doors to his laboratory in Menlo Park, New Jersey, and introduced the incandescent electric light bulb to the people. More than 3,000 people came to see Edison's laboratory, office, home, and the grounds around these buildings lit up by electric lamps.

(right) On January 27, 1880, Thomas Edison was granted U.S. Patent 223,898 for his incandescent electric light bulb.

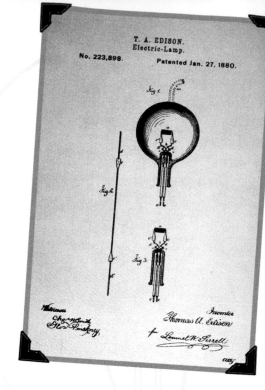

T. A. EDISON.
Electric-Lamp.
No. 223,898.   Patented Jan. 27, 1880.

16

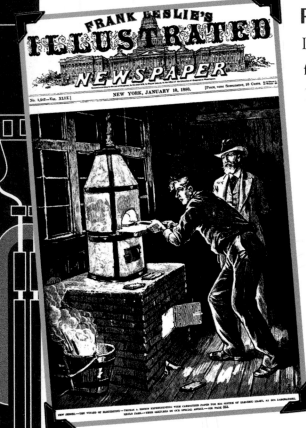

FRANK LESLIE'S ILLUSTRATED NEWSPAPER

NEW YORK, JANUARY 10, 1880.

Public Reaction

In 1880, the Edison Electric Light Company, which had been founded two years earlier, installed light bulbs on a ship, in New York City office buildings, and in the homes of a few wealthy people. While some people thought the new lights were unnatural, most were amazed that they did not flicker or give off as much heat as torches or candles. A few people were suspicious of electric lights, mainly because they thought that electricity, such as that created during lightning storms, was dangerous. When a town in Illinois installed electric lights in 1885, farmers outside the town mistook the glow for fire. They rushed in on wagons to help fight the blaze.

(left) In the weeks after Thomas Edison opened his laboratory to the public, newspapers and magazines were full of stories about Edison and his electric light.

1600	1705	1746	1800	1807	1850
William Gilbert uses the word "electric" to describe static electricity.	Francis Hauksbee invents the first machine to generate static electricity.	Pieter van Musschenbroek invents the Leyden jar, allowing electricity to be stored.	Alessandro Volta invents the first modern battery and generates a steady current of electricity.	Humphry Davy invents the arc lamp, the first usable electric light.	The first electric arc light system is installed in the Paris Opera House.

Convincing the Public

Scientists, politicians, and especially **insurance companies** helped
Edison convince the public that electric lights were going to benefit
people. Insurance companies paid out money to people when their
houses or other buildings burned down. Insurance companies offered
discounts, or cheaper payments, to businesses that installed electric
lighting systems because they were safer than torches, candles, or oil
lamps. Across North America, theaters were lit with electric lights,
and actors wore electric lights on their costumes. Electricity displays,
organized by Edison's company, as well as town and city councils,
appeared at country and city fairs to help people understand electric
lights. In 1892, Edison paid for an "electricity" float in the popular
New York City parade. Electrical companies such as Edison's placed
advertisements that had flashing lights of different colors and sizes
in the streets and on the sides of buildings. They also placed stencil
drawings over light bulbs and projected the images onto clouds.

(above) In 1893, the
Electrical Building at
the World's
Columbian Exposition
in Chicago drew
thousands of people
to see electric lights.
Demonstrations
helped people
understand the
new invention.

1879	1910	1950s	1960s	1970s	1991	2000s
Joseph Swan and Thomas Edison each demonstrate their incandescent light bulbs.	William David Coolidge's tungsten metal filament increases the light bulb's energy efficiency.	Tungsten halogen lamps are invented.	Fluorescent light bulbs replace incandescent light bulbs in most public places.	Mass production of LED lights begins.	The first HID headlights and taillights appear on cars.	Compact, energy-efficient fluorescent lights become widely available.

Changing Lives

At first, electricity was very expensive, and only the wealthiest people in North America and Europe could afford it. As electricity became more common and prices dropped, and as people became more accustomed to the new invention, more electric lights were installed in homes and workplaces.

Out at Night

Electric lights created brighter illumination than candles and oil lamps, so people could see better at night. With electric lights, cooking, cleaning, reading, and entertaining guests in the evening were all much easier. Streetlights were installed in more American cities and towns, making people feel safer after night fell. In 1895, in Jacksonville, Florida, city officials declared that they needed fewer police officers. They believed that the bright lights would prevent people from committing crimes at night.

(above) Lights illuminated the Plaza hotel and other buildings in New York City in the 1880s.

(below) With electric light, events such as baseball games could take place after dark.

Electrifying America

With the success of the electric light bulb, electricity began to be used for other purposes, especially to power machines. In 1890, in London, England, electric subways replaced subways powered by steam and coal. In the 1920s, televisions powered by electricity replaced mechanical televisions. By the early 1930s, ovens and refrigerators, which are both powered by electricity, had replaced wood or coal cook stoves and ice boxes in most homes.

New Jobs

The new electrical industry created thousands of jobs. Electricians installed electric lights, workers ran electrical generating stations, and professors and teachers trained people in the new science of electricity. Electricity also changed the way jobs were done. Electric lights allowed workers to work longer into the night, while machines powered by electricity, including electric sewing machines and printing presses, often did jobs faster and more efficiently than people, sometimes replacing them.

(above) In large electric light factories, employees made thousands of light bulbs every day.

(above) This advertisement from the International Electric Exhibition in London, England, in 1882, shows the many uses of electricity.

Improving Light

The incandescent electric light bulb has changed since Joseph Swan and Thomas Edison invented it over 100 years ago. These changes have improved the bulb's brightness, and life span, or how long it lasts. Despite the changes, incandescent light bulbs today still work on the same basic principle as early light bulbs.

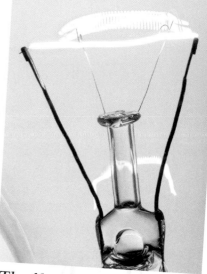

The filament is the part of the light bulb that glows. When the filament breaks apart, the light bulb burns out.

Filaments

Inventors other than Edison and Swan also experimented with different filaments to get more light from light bulbs using the same amount of power. In 1882, American inventor Lewis Latimer patented a process for making pure carbon filaments. His filaments were easier to make and did not break as easily as other types. In the United States, Willis Whitney also experimented with carbon filaments, baking them at extremely high temperatures so that they incandesced more efficiently.

Other scientists, including American William David Coolidge, looked for ways to make light bulbs burn brighter and more efficiently. In the early 1900s, Coolidge was one of the first people to use a filament made of tungsten, a type of metal. Tungsten can withstand very high temperatures without catching fire or melting, which is important since filaments are heated to around 4,500° Fahrenheit (2,482° Celsius). Tungsten filaments are still used in light bulbs today.

William David Coolidge, on the right, and Irving Langmuir, on the left, were both very well-known scientists, partly because of their work on different parts of electric light.

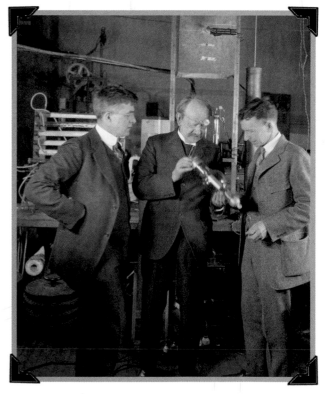

Inert Gas

In 1910, an American chemist named Irving Langmuir discovered that filling a light bulb with an **inert** gas allows the tungsten to operate at higher temperatures, turning more electricity into light. By 1913, incandescent tungsten lamps filled with an inert gas were for sale. Today, all incandescent light bulbs are filled with an inert gas, such as argon, instead of being emptied of air like Swan's and Edison's first bulbs.

Higher-watt bulbs have longer and thicker filaments, so they consume more energy and produce more light. This light bulb uses 100 watts of electricity to produce its light.

Greater Energy Efficiency

Light bulbs are made and sold based on how much energy they consume. The amount of electrical power going into a light bulb is measured in watts. Light bulbs give off different amounts of light, measured in lumens. It is important to be able to have different amounts of light in different places, since some tasks, such as reading, require brighter light than other tasks.

The majority of electricity that light bulbs use is actually wasted as heat. Only a very small part of the electricity helps produce the light that humans can see. Since the 1880s, scientists and engineers have tried to improve the light bulb's energy efficiency, or how much electricity is used to produce a given amount of light. Energy efficiency is measured in lumens per watt.

Different Colors, Sizes, and Shapes

After Edison introduced his light bulb to the public, inventors and electric light companies began to make bulbs in different sizes and shapes. They made bulbs the size of people for parade floats and electrical shows, and tiny bulbs that could be worn on clothes or even in women's hair. Bulbs for chandeliers were shaped like the flames of candles, and other shapes were designed to fit stylish lamps and fixtures. Inventors and electric light companies also coated glass bulbs with different color dyes, so that the bulbs glowed the color of the dye instead of their usual yellowish color.

Colored bulbs illuminate stages in theaters, decorate halls and outdoor spaces, and are hung on Christmas trees.

Inside a Light Bulb

Billions of incandescent light bulbs are used around the world. Most last for 750 hours before burning out. Some incandescent bulbs used for photography last only six hours, whereas other bulbs, such as those used to explore dark caves, last for 3,000 hours.

1. Electrical foot contact: The electrical foot contact brings electricity into the light bulb. When a light bulb in a lamp is turned on, an electric current flows from the lamp's electrical foot contact to the light bulb's electrical foot contact.

2. Base: The base of a bulb is where the contact with electricity is made. It is made out of metal to conduct the electricity. The base is threaded so that light bulbs can be screwed securely into lamps and light fixtures.

3. Glass mount: The glass mount is a very thin piece of glass that supports the lead wires and the filament.

4. Lead wires: The lead wires carry the electric current between the foot contact and the filament.

5. Filament: The filament is the part of the light bulb that incandesces when heated by electricity. It is a thin piece of tungsten metal 21 feet (6.5 meters) long. In a typical light bulb, the filament is wound up in a coil less than one inch (2.5 centimeters) long.

6. Anchor wires: Anchor wires hold the filament in place.

7. Glass bulb: The glass bulb is filled with an inert gas, usually argon, to make the electric light more efficient. Most glass bulbs for electric lights in homes are frosted on the inside with a type of acid. The acid reduces the glare, or the harshness of the light. Dyes, **phosphors**, or colored glass are used to make the color of the light appear less yellow.

Switch

The electric current runs through a light switch. Flipping on the switch closes the electrical circuit. Electricity runs through the switch, to the light bulb, back to the switch, and to the ground to complete the circuit. Turning off the switch opens, or breaks, the circuit, preventing electricity from reaching the light bulb.

New Light Bulbs

Most light bulbs in the home are an improved version of Edison's first electric light bulb. Today, other types of electric light bulbs are used to produce different kinds of light to meet specific needs.

Fluorescent Lights

Alexandre-Edmond Becquerel, a French physicist, demonstrated the fluorescent light bulb in 1867. The first practical fluorescent light bulbs were developed in the United States in the 1930s, by teams working at two electrical companies — Westinghouse and the General Electric Company.

Fluorescent light bulbs do not have a filament. Instead, they are filled with gas and **mercury**, and the insides are coated with a white powder called a phosphor. When an electric current passes through the bulb, it heats up the mercury, which emits, or gives off, a type of light called ultraviolet light. Humans cannot see ultraviolet light, but it causes the phosphor to fluoresce, or glow brightly, creating visible light. Fluorescent light bulbs last longer than normal incandescent light bulbs. They are also more energy efficient.

Neon Lights

French chemist and engineer Georges Claude studied inert gases while working in the fuel industry. He created the first electric light that used a type of gas called neon in 1902, and displayed it to the public in 1910. Like fluorescent lights, neon lights produce light when the gas particles they contain are exposed to an electric current. When the current flows through the tube, the gases convert, or change, some of the energy into light.

Until recently, fluorescent lights were mostly used in public workplaces, such as schools and hospitals. Today, compact fluorescent bulbs, such as the one above, are used in homes.

Neon-Style Bulbs

Neon gas produces a red light, so bulbs filled with neon glow bright red. Other neon-style bulbs use different gases, such as mercury or helium. Mercury produces a blue light, while helium produces a gold light. Some tubes are coated with phosphors that produce different colors when they react with electrified gases.

(right) The most popular use for neon lights is for advertising, such as these bright signs on the streets of Shanghai, China.

(above) Halogen lamps are very bright, but they are currently only strong enough to light up small areas.

Halogen Lamps

In 1953, American scientist Elmer Fridrich developed a **halogen** lamp while working for the General Electric Company. Some of Fridrich's lamps worked well, but others did not work at all. In 1954, General Electric assigned scientist Edward Zubler to figure out what was going wrong inside Fridrich's lamps. In 1959, Zubler's team of scientists made halogen lamps that worked well.

Halogen lamps are a type of incandescent light bulb. They have a tungsten filament, but are filled with a halogen gas, usually iodine or bromine, instead of an inert gas. When electrified, the filament has a chemical reaction with the gas that allows the filament to burn at a very high temperature without falling apart or melting. The greater heat makes the light from halogen lamps brighter than light from ordinary incandescent bulbs. This greater heat would break glass bulbs, so halogen bulbs are made either from quartz, which is a clear mineral that can withstand high temperatures, or from a type of high-strength glass known as "hard glass."

Lighting a City

Once Thomas Edison invented his light bulb, he needed a way to generate electricity for more than just his laboratory and home. Edison's first generating station opened on Pearl Street in New York City in 1882. It produced enough electricity to light up more than 24 office buildings. Today, a single generating station can light up thousands of buildings.

Generators

Michael Faraday was Humphry Davy's assistant, and he experimented with electricity throughout his life. In 1821, Faraday observed that an electric current passing through a wire caused a magnet near the wire to move. He also discovered that moving a strong magnet quickly between the coils of a wire generated an electric current in the wire.

Faraday used this knowledge to build the first electrical generator, or a machine that produces a continuous, strong, steady current of electricity. He demonstrated his generator in 1831 in London. Faraday's generator was the first generator able to produce enough electricity to power factories. It is the basis of all generators, both large and small, used today.

Edison's Pearl Street generators were powered by steam. Early generating stations were loud, hot, and dangerous places to work because of the risk of electrocution, or being killed by electricity.

Hydroelectric generators such as these are powered by falling water. Other generators are driven by steam, produced either by a nuclear reactor or by burning fossil fuels, such as coal and oil.

Moving Electricity

Once electricity is generated in a central power station, it flows along a network of wires, called transmission lines, to a substation. In a substation, a device called a transformer reduces the voltage, or strength, of the electricity before it flows into buildings. The voltage must be lowered so that the electrical equipment does not short-circuit, or break.

Power Failures

Many people have experienced power failures, or times when the electricity has suddenly gone out. Most power failures occur when transmission lines break due to heavy wind, rain, or snow, and the electricity cannot get to where it is needed. Power failures also result from problems in a central power station, such as generators overheating and breaking down.

AC/DC

Electric currents can travel in different ways. A direct current (DC) moves in one direction only, and loses strength as it travels over distances. An alternating current (AC) can flow in either direction, and can travel farther without losing much of its strength. Thomas Edison's electrical system used a direct current. When Nikola Tesla, a scientist who once worked for Edison, devised a system for generating and transmitting electric current in 1887, he used alternating current. For the rest of their lives, Edison and Tesla disagreed over which system was better.

Edison believed that a direct current was safer because it could not shock a person as badly as an alternating current. Tesla argued that an alternating current was more practical because it lost less power and the voltage could be adjusted, depending on a building's needs. Today, most modern electrical systems use a mix of AC and DC. DC is used in batteries and to power elevators, subways, and some very heavy electrical motors.

Specialized Uses

Once the science behind electric light was discovered, light bulbs were adapted for different purposes. They began to be used in movie projectors, to show films; in camera flashes, so that people could take pictures in dark places; in refrigerators, so that people could see the food inside; and in many other places and devices.

Safety on the Roads

The first automobile with electric lights was made in 1898. Electric lights on cars help drivers see the road ahead, other vehicles, and pedestrians. Lights are also used on other vehicles, such as bicycles, snowmobiles, and motorboats. All these vehicles use special bulbs that last a very long time.

Traffic lights are electric lights that make road intersections safer for cars and pedestrians. Before traffic lights were invented, traffic signals consisted of t-shaped poles with signs for Stop, Go, and All Stop, which stopped traffic in all directions so pedestrians could cross the street. A timer controlled the signal changes, as it does in electric traffic lights today. Many road signs use tiny lights arranged to form different patterns or words. Overhead signs on highways tell drivers about traffic and weather conditions ahead. On roads with construction, signs with flashing arrows show drivers where workers are working, and direct traffic into other lanes.

People who work in dark conditions use electric lights to see what they are doing. Miners use small, battery-powered electric lights that are lightweight, very bright, and often attach to the fronts of their helmets. Archaeologists and cave explorers also use these lights when exploring underground areas or other dark places.

Security

Paper money, credit cards, and important documents, such as passports, are often made with special designs, or marks, called watermarks. These watermarks are created with a substance that can only be seen using a special light source, known as a black light lamp. Black light lamps produce ultraviolet light, which the human eye cannot see directly but which makes otherwise invisible things, such as watermarks, glow. Black light lamps are also used by crime scene investigators to check for evidence, such as blood or saliva.

In this black light theater show, performers hold puppets painted with special black light paint. The puppets glow in the dark when exposed to black light lamps.

High-powered electric lights on submersibles, or underwater vehicles, illuminate the dark ocean. They help scientists study life under water and discover new kinds of fish, water insects, and plants.

Medicine

Electric lights are used in hospitals in various ways. In operating rooms, high-powered electric light bulbs provide a very bright light that allows doctors to see better during surgery. Doctors also use light to help diagnose illnesses without cutting patients open. Tiny light bulbs and cameras are attached to fiber optic cables, or extremely thin cables made of glass. The cables can twist and bend to reach different areas inside the body, and the images they send back to monitors are bright and extremely clear. Babies born with jaundice, a common condition of the liver that turns the skin yellow, are placed under special electric lights that cure the condition.

Light Tomorrow

E lectric light bulbs first amazed people less than 150 years ago. Now, they are a necessary part of life for most people. Scientists today are working to make brighter, less expensive, more energy-efficient lights. With so many people now using electricity, conserving energy is more important than ever before.

HID Lamps

High Intensity Discharge (HID) lamps and light bulbs were invented in the early 1900s. They produce a very bright light and use less power than most fluorescent bulbs. HID bulbs are filled with gases and metals. When electricity enters the bulb, an arc is created between two small tungsten electrodes, which heats up the gas. The gas heats the other metals, causing them to emit light. One disadvantage of HID lamps is that they take between three and five minutes to light up to their full power, and they have to stay off for 10 to 15 minutes before they can be turned on again. Scientists are trying to reduce the time it takes for HID lamps to turn on and cool down by experimenting with different materials, metals, and gases.

(above) HID lights are used in some underwater video cameras, because they illuminate a larger area more clearly than other lights.

(left) HID lamps light large spaces, such as warehouses, gymnasiums, baseball stadiums, and amusement parks.

LED Lights

Light-emitting diode (LED) lights are used in the displays of clock radios and DVD players, in computer and television screens, in exit signs in buildings, and on electronic billboard advertisements. They were developed in the 1950s, and became common in the 1970s. LED lights do not use glass bulbs or filaments. They are made from tiny bits of specially made metals and are covered with a protective plastic. When electrons move from one metal to another, they produce light. LED lights last much longer than many other types of light bulbs, and are more energy efficient than incandescent bulbs.

More Lights

Scientists and engineers are looking for ways to bring light to more parts of the world. They are trying to find less expensive ways to generate electricity, and are developing generating machines that will work in places with extreme weather conditions. Scientists and engineers are also exploring ways to power extremely large areas without transmission lines and **power grids**, which would be very difficult and expensive to install.

Scientists are working on ways to make LED technology less expensive and are adapting LED lights so that they can be used for general lighting.

Reducing Pollution

Many scientists are working to make electric light bulbs more energy efficient, or able to produce the same amount of light using less electricity. They are also trying to find ways to generate electricity that do not involve burning fossil fuels, which causes pollution. Electrical generators are sometimes powered with wind and water, and electricity is sometimes generated using solar cells, specially coated panels of glass that catch the Sun's rays. Scientists are working to make these environmentally friendly electrical generators less expensive and more powerful.

Wind turbines provide power to power grids, which then provide electricity to homes and other buildings.

Glossary

acid A chemical, or group of chemicals, that is sour-tasting and can be dissolved in water

amber A hard yellow, orange, or light brown fossilized substance from ancient trees

archaeologist A person who studies the past by examining buildings and artifacts

barometer An instrument used in weather forecasting to measure changes in the pressure of the atmosphere

carbon A chemical element found in all living things, and also comes in the form of graphite, charcoal, and coal

carbonize To coat with carbon

charcoal A substance made from a carbon material, such as wood or another organic, or once living, material

dissection To cut something apart for scientific investigation

electrode An electricity conductor, such as a terminal on a battery, through which electricity can flow in or out

fossil fuel A fuel, such as coal or natural gas, that is made from the remains of plants or animals

fuse A device that protects from a circuit overload by opening, or breaking, the electrical current

halogen Any of the elements fluorine, chlorine, iodine, bromine, or astatine

inert Slow to react chemically

insurance companies Businesses that receive regular payments from customers and then pay money to their customers if their property is damaged

magnetism The force associated with magnets and electrical currents

matter Anything that has mass and takes up space

mercury A heavy, metallic chemical element that is liquid at room temperature

nuclear reactor A device in which atoms are split to produce heat. The heat is often used to generate power

patent A document that is meant to prevent, for a certain number of years, other people from copying an inventor's idea without permission and without paying a fee

particles Very small pieces of things

philosopher A person who tries to answer questions about truth, right and wrong, God, and the meaning of life

phosphor A material that glows when hit by electrons

prehistoric The period of time in history before written records were kept

power grid A system of cables that distribute electricity throughout an area

resin A yellow or light brown substance that comes from the sap of some trees and plants

zinc A silvery metal

Index

32

Printed in the U.S.A.